P9-DWG-974

HARCOURT BRACE & COMPANY

SAN DIEGO   NEW YORK   LONDON

THE BALLYMARA FLOOD

WRITTEN BY

CHAD STUART

ILLUSTRATED BY

GEORGE BOOTH

In Ireland ballads are commonly sung to the tune of a
jig. For best effect when reading aloud, the reader is
advised to attempt an Irish accent and to bear in mind
the jig's lilting rhythm.

Text copyright © 1996 by Chad Stuart
Illustrations copyright © 1996 by George Booth

Library of Congress Cataloging-in-Publication Data
Stuart, Chad.
The Ballymara flood/by Chad Stuart;
illustrated by George Booth. — 1st ed.
p.   cm.
Summary: Pandemonium reigns when a boy's bathtub overflows
and floods the Irish town of Ballymara.
ISBN 0-15-205698-X
[1. Floods—Fiction. 2. Ireland—Fiction. 3. Humorous stories.
4. Stories in rhyme.] I. Booth, George, 1926-   ill. II. Title.
PZ8.3.S916Bal   1996
[E]—dc20   94-15162

First edition
A B C D E

Printed in Singapore

For my children, and everyone else's, too — C. S.

To Sarah's grandmother — G. B.

Once upon a time there was
A very famous case
Of a boy in Ballymara town
Who flooded out the place.

He didn't want to have a wash;
His mother made him do it.
She locked him in the bathroom,
And she told him to get to it.

Higgledy piggledy hi-de-ho,
The boy got in the tub.
Reluctantly, he took the soap,
And he began to scrub.

He tried to turn the water off,
But he was out of luck.
He pulled and tugged and pushed and shoved;
The faucets—they were stuck.

He banged upon the bathroom door.
"Hey, Mother, turn the key!"
His mother never heard him;
She was watching the TV.

Higgledy piggledy hi-de-ho,
The water poured and poured.
It came up to his knees and burst
Right through the bathroom door!

The stairs became a waterfall,
And much to her dismay,
His mother missed her program
As the TV sailed away.

She sent the lad to fetch his dad;
The boy ran very hard.
But when they both came dashing home,
The water filled the yard!

Higgledy piggledy hi-de-ho,
The water rose much higher.
So Dad went to the garden shed
To fetch a pair of pliers.

But when Dad tried to climb the stairs,
The flood washed him away.
He hit his head, and then he said,
"What will the neighbors say?"

"We have to find the main," he gasped,
And waded down the hall.
The stop-valve came off in his hands,
Which did no good at all.

Higgledy piggledy hi-de-ho,
The water reached the street.
The neighbors had to go about
With waders on their feet.

The father shouted to his son,
"Look what a mess you've made!"
He struggled through the living room
And called the fire brigade.

The fire brigade came down the hill
And got a terrible shock.
They crashed into the baker's van
As they tore around the block.

Higgledy piggledy hi-de-ho,
The flood was pouring down.
And pretty soon, by the afternoon,
The water had reached the town.

The fireman telephoned the mayor,
Who took it very hard.
He chewed his pencil into bits
And called the national guard.

He cried out, "Help! Emergency!
You've got to save us here!"
The army sent a rescue team,
The corps of engineers.

Higgledy piggledy hi-de-ho,
The flood began to rise.
The people had to move upstairs,
Much to their great surprise.

The soldiers came in jeeps and trucks,
And army transport planes.
They brought so many people there,
They blocked the country lanes!

The mayor called up the navy, too,
And he began to plead,
"We cannot last! We're sinking fast!
I think it's boats we need!"

Higgledy piggledy hi-de-ho,
The water came pouring down.
The Ballymara reservoir
Was filling up the town.

The admiral was very nice
And sent a rescue fleet.
They made a splendid sight to see,
All sailing down the street.

The folks in Ballymara town
Thought it was very strange.
They were fishing from their windows,
And that made quite a change.

Higgledy piggledy hi-de-ho,
They made a terrible fuss
Because they had to board a boat
Instead of take the bus.

The corps of engineers set out
To find the reservoir.
They said they'd fix the problem
And be back in half an hour.

But they returned with faces red,
Embarrassed as could be.
They left in such a hurry,
They forgot to take the key.

Higgledy piggledy hi-de-ho,
The key was never there.
The guard was away on holiday,
And he hadn't left a spare!

The mayor convened a meeting
On the roof of city hall.
"The situation's very grave,"
He said to one and all.

"Now some of you may wish to stay;
Some may choose to quit.
And if you want to give up now,
I won't blame you one bit."

Higgledy piggledy hi-de-ho,
They voted to remain.
"Without a doubt, we'll stick it out;
Let's hope it doesn't rain!"

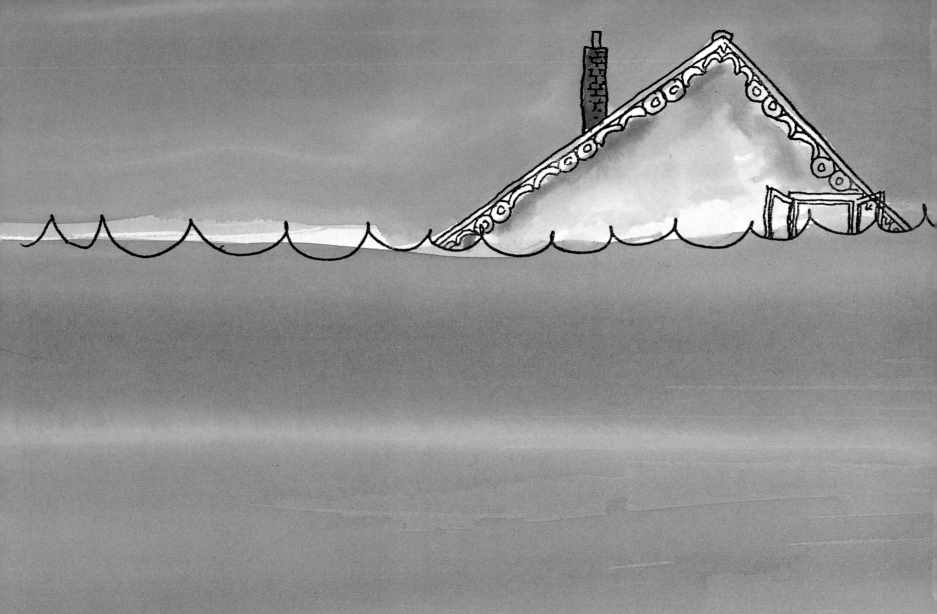

The boy was feeling very bad;
He knew it was his fault.
He tried to think what he could do
To bring things to a halt.

So late that night, he found a wrench.
He took a boat as well.
And stealthily he rowed it past
The Royal Arms Hotel.

Higgledy piggledy hi-de-ho,
He rowed up to his house.
He didn't wake the neighbors;
He was quiet as a mouse.

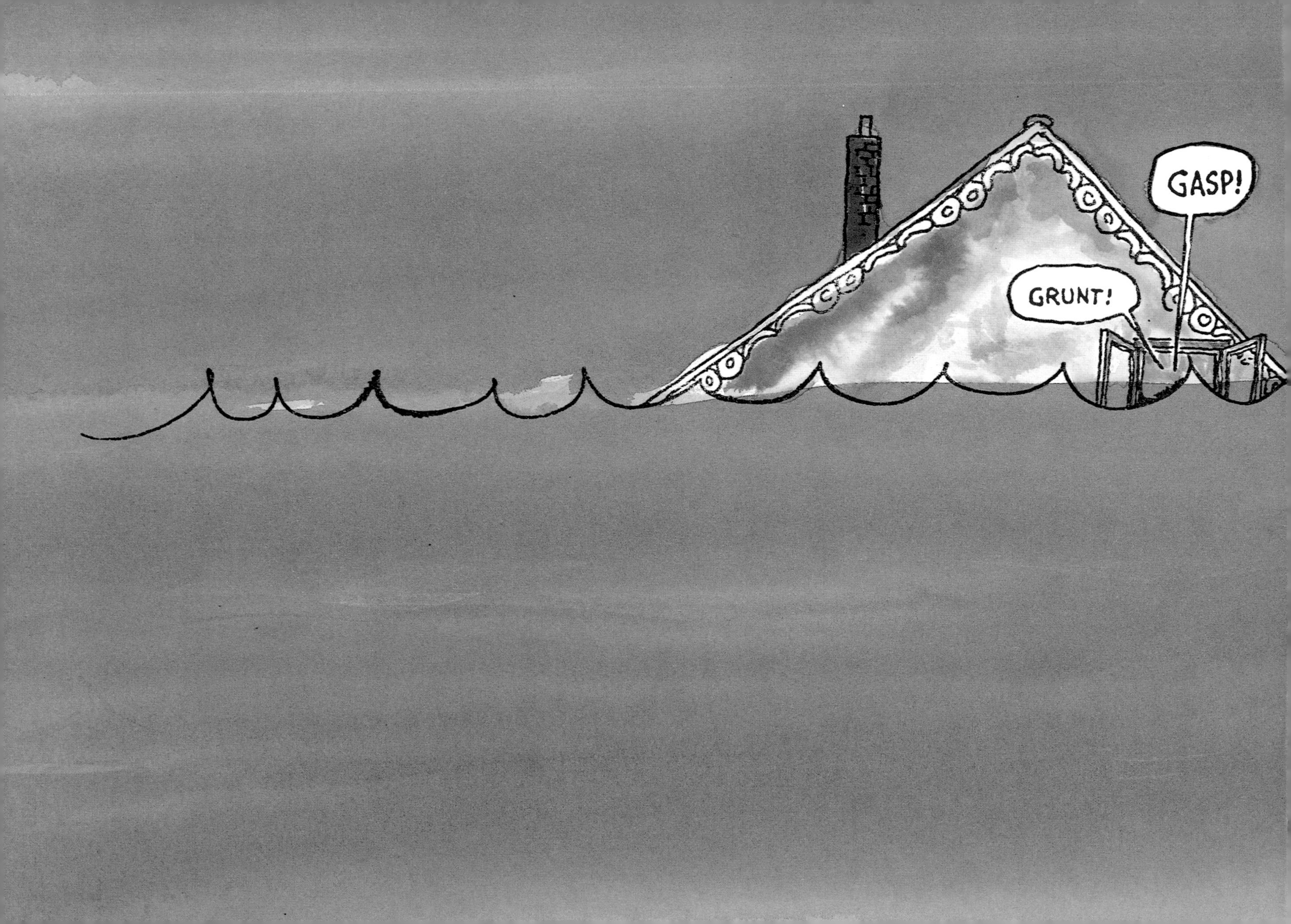
GRUNT!
GASP!

He found the bathroom window,
And he opened it with ease.
Then cautiously he clambered in
Upon his hands and knees.

He shone his flashlight round the room;
It was a fearful sight.
He grabbed the wrench and went to work,
And pulled with all his might.

Higgledy piggledy hi-de-ho,
He grunted and he gasped.
To his relief, the faucets turned;
The water stopped at last!

The lad became a hero,
And that was only right,
For by himself, he saved the day
With what he did that night.

It was a very simple plan,
And simply carried through.
It's strange he was the only one
Who thought of what to do.

Higgledy piggledy hi-de-ho,
The water ebbed away.
The mayor was so relieved that he
Declared a holiday.

He organized a big parade,
With ice cream and a band.
The boy was guest of honor,
And he shook the mayor's hand.

They gave the lad a medal
To commemorate the day
When all of Ballymara town
Was nearly washed away.

Higgledy piggledy hi-de-ho,
They all marched through the mud.
Now every year they raise a cheer
For the Ballymara flood!

The illustrations in this book were done in pen-and-ink and watercolor
on Arches watercolor paper.
The display type was set in Las Bonitas.
The text type was set in Cochin.
Color separations by Bright Arts, Ltd., Singapore
Printed and bound by Tien Wah Press, Singapore
This book was printed with soya-based inks on Leykam recycled paper,
which contains more than 20 percent postconsumer waste and has a
total recycled content of at least 50 percent.
Production supervision by Warren Wallerstein and Pascha Gerlinger
Designed by Linda Lockowitz

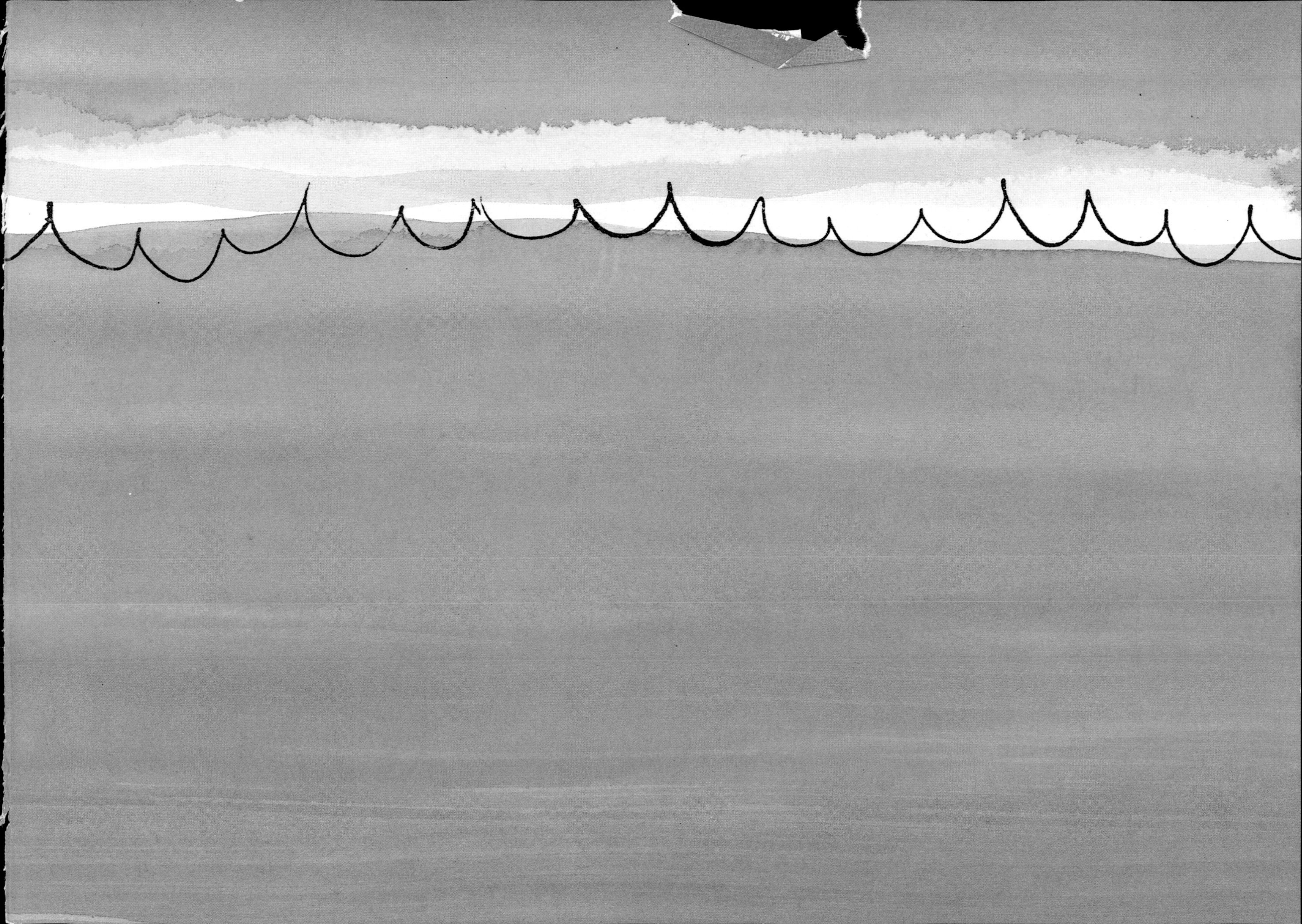